THE POWER

By Ginny Seymour

Cover Illustrator
Tammy C Dickson

Evensong Publishing

THE POWER
Copyright @ 1999
All Rights reserved
Printed in the United States of America
Library of Congress TX 5-633-879
ISBN 0-9718325-2-8

TABLE OF CONTENTS

TRAINING MANUAL FOR LAND OWNERSHIP

Receive the Power - a Word from the Author
THE CURTAIN RISES

CHAPTER ONE   **POWER IN THE KINGDOM**................... 3
           Worship in the Spirit............................ 7
           Gifts of the Holy Spirit...............................8
CHAPTER TWO   **KNOW THE ENEMY**......................... 10
           Forbidden Practices: Occult and Cults.... 13
CHAPTER THREE **PREPARE FOR BATTLE**....................... 15
           Take a Stand... 17
           The Suit of Light...................................... 19
CHAPTER FOUR **TOOLS OF WARFARE**......................... 23
           Music, Praise, Worship and Laughter....... 24
           Scripture..25
           The Secret Code - The Color Star........... 26
CHAPTER FIVE   **TAKE THE LAND**................................. 28
           Names of Evil Spirits.............................. 29
           Name Above All Names......................... 30
           The Lying Spirit...................................... 32
           The Haughty Spirit and Spirit of Infirmity.... 33
           Spirit of Perversion and Spirit of Rebellion.34
           Spirit of Heaviness and Spirit of Fear........35
           Spirit of Jealousy 36
           Deaf and Dumb Spirit............................37
           Spirit of Whoredom............................... 38
           Spirit of Bondage and Spirit of Anti-Christ. 39
           Spirits that Cause Division........................ 41
           Spirits of Insanity - Unteachable Spirit...... 45
           The Spirits that Cause Apostasy.............. 48
           The Heart of the Chart......................... 50
REVIEW   **THE COLOR OF THE LIE**..................... 52
CHAPTER SIX   **EXODUS JOURNAL**........................ 55-70
           The Last Word - Pastor MaryJo Lovelady..71

Believe the Power

Believe the Power

The Power is revolutionary in approach as it exposes the native language of the enemy. It is the only text showing how demonic spirits are related through color, number and the voice they speak. There are individual charts to color to help you recognize evil spirits and how they relate and directions to help you in your journey to freedom.

This is a handbook for land ownership. First you learn to take back your own land. This land is the body, soul and spirit of man. When the spirit of man has been entrapped by the enemy, it has an effect on the body and soul. To free the spirit demands taking authority over demonic forces. It is a process of deliverance. Once you have set yourself free, you can free others.

This text reveals how the Holy Spirit operates through the nine gifts of the Spirit, the nine fruits of the Spirit and the nine areas of deliverance. Nine is the number representing the Holy Spirit. The enemy can only work out of the pattern established by God and so there are many manifestations of spirits but only nine ruling evil spirits.

The Holy Spirit is the third person of the triune God, the power source revealing the strategies behind enemy lines. He leads you into all Kingdom understanding. He is the Spirit of truth, revelation and power! Ask Him to guide you and give you the wisdom as you learn. Now is the time to walk in God's Glory and receive His Power!

I wish to especially thank Tammy Dickson for encouraging me to complete this huge "God project". Now I pray for you, the reader: *that the eyes of your heart might be enlightened in order that you may know the hope to which He has called you, the riches of His glorious inheritance in the saints, and His incomparably great power for us who believe.*

For the Kingdom, the Glory and the Power! Ginny Seymour

Note: All Scripture references are from the NIV Study Bible.

.

THE CURTAIN RISES

Imagine an audience in a crowded, dimly-lit theater. Old Father Mike, a Catholic priest from the old country, wonders why he decided to take in a movie tonight. Occasionally his head droops in sleep. He shakes himself awake and again wonders why he is not home sitting in his tattered easy chair working on tomorrow's homily.

In the balcony, Baptist kids whisper and giggle. Some prim Pentecostals perch to the right of the center aisle. To the left of the center aisle sit a smattering of animated, noisy Charismatics. In the reserve section a cluster of Lutherans and Episcopalians munch on popcorn.

Folk from every Christian persuasion are represented, including, in the far back, almost completely hidden from view, a solitary Methodist. The audience falls silent as the theater lights fade and envelop them in darkness.

Slowly, the great, golden drape begins to rise. Glorious waves of praise sweep the stage and break upon the audience.

The sound of praise, like the pounding seas during a storm, rises to a greater intensity as each fold of the curtain moves higher. The opening curtain reveals a massive door hanging upon the gate posts of heaven. The wave of praise ebbs but a sweet fragrance lingers. Trumpets blare in the distance.

A sudden, loud clap of thunder shakes the theater.

Father Mike jolts awake. Popcorn is forgotten by the Lutherans and Episcopalians and the noisy Charismatics are suddenly silenced. The Baptist children lean forward in great expectation. The solitary Methodist leaves his seat to inch cautiously forward for a closer look.

A huge bolt of lightening rips across the theater and touches down right in front of the curious Methodist. Thunder follows. The little theater shakes. The Methodist quickly scurries back to his seat and to safety. Before the Methodist can settle himself in, the massive double doors on stage begin to open.

Bright shining lights shoot out from the crack in the

opening doors. Shafts of light sweep the audience. Father Mike shades his eyes with his hand as the doors continue to open. Shards of dazzling lights, swirling clouds and flashes of lightning frame the great doorway. The voices of many thunders resound.

The open doorway floods the little theater with the brilliant lights. The lights of shining angels - tens of thousands of them. The angels ascend upwards out of sight into blazing, glorious color. Black storm clouds rage! Trumpets blare! The Angels descend! Lightening rips across the stage. Thunder booms! The little theater shudders. The golden drape drops.

ACT II

Once again there is wave-upon-wave of praise. A muted trumpet sounds. The golden drape moves aside to reveal the massive door. The great door stands open. Inside is now only a great, blue, quiet portal.

ACT III

Father Mike stands up, stretches and then shuffles between the seats and back up the aisle. Unseen, two, towering, warrior angels follow close behind him. Under the arm of each angel is a large glowing book.

The Baptist children exit the theater. A host of guardian angels, each carrying large books, trail behind them.

And so it goes until the theater empties its' cargo into the streets. Each one exits accompanied by angels. Each angel carries a large, glowing, golden book.

To those with ears to hear, let them hear what the Spirit is saying to believers:

There is a paradigm shift in the spirit world!
Angels are being dispensed!
God is assigning orders to His end time army!

<u>Training Manual for Land Ownership</u>

1
Power in the Kingdom

When Jesus was baptized in the river Jordan by John the Baptist, the Holy Spirit descended upon Him (Luke 3:21). Until that point in history, Scripture does not record one miracle Jesus performed in all of His thirty years. From that moment the life of Jesus was filled with dynamite. He taught with power, healed with power and delivered with power! He had been filled with the Holy Spirit. This is the model for our lives.

And I will send the Holy Spirit to lead you into all truth and He will teach you all things (John 14:26).

After the resurrection of Jesus, Jesus instructed His disciples to wait in Jerusalem and He would invest them with the Holy Spirit and with power. These signs were to follow those who believe: they would drive out demons, speak with new tongues, pick up snakes and not be harmed, drink deadly poison and not be harmed and place their hands on the sick and the sick would recover (Matthew 28:18-20, Mark 16:15-18, Luke 46-49 and Acts 1:4-8).

If you are a believer, these signs follow you! There is no room for argument. If you are a believer these signs must follow.

Scripture could not be more concise. Believers receive this power from the Holy Spirit the same way Jesus did.

The disciples, in a group totaling about 120, along with Mary, the mother of Jesus, waited and stayed in constant prayer. Suddenly the Holy Spirit descended. ...like the blowing of a violent wind from heaven and filled the whole house where they were sitting. They saw what seemed to be tongues of fire that separated and came to rest on each of them. All of them were filled with the Holy Spirit and began to speak in other tongues (Acts 2:2-4).

The disciples turned from mice into lions in the blink of an eye. From that moment of time the disciples preached, healed and delivered people all in the Name of Jesus. They had become powerhouses of faith. They personally experienced the Holy Spirit.

Scripture encourages us to be filled with the Spirit and to expect the Holy Spirit as part of the average life of a believer (Mark 1:8, Mark 8:15, John 1:33, John 20:22, Acts 1:5-8, 2:4, 8:15, 9:17, 11:16, 19:24 and Ephesians 5:18). The word for power mentioned in the coming of the Holy Spirit in (Acts) means dynamite. Once touched with this dynamite, a believer is empowered to live the Christian experience.

Jesus said, "I tell you the truth, no one can see the Kingdom of God unless he is born again."

Nicodemus asked. "How can a man be born again when he is old? Surely he cannot enter a second time into his mother's womb?"

Jesus answered, "I tell you the truth, no one can enter the Kingdom of God unless he is born of water and the Spirit. Flesh gives birth to flesh but the Spirit gives birth to spirit" (John 3:3-5).

As a Christian you have experienced the first birth, which is Salvation. Salvation is usually followed soon after by water baptism. The second birth is being born of the Spirit. When you are born of the Spirit, it is rather like an experience of being born. You become born to see with new eyes, to hear with new ears and to walk in the supernatural realm. Now and then Salvation and the infilling of the Holy Spirit happens at the same time. Receiving either is not a matter of works, nor a matter of our goodness nor a matter of who we are. These are free gifts of the Kingdom.

If Jesus is your Savior, and you have had the Salvation experience, then how do you enter into the experience with the Holy Spirit? The Holy Spirit already resides in every Christian who accepts Jesus into their heart. When you accepted Jesus into your heart, you accepted God the Father, the Son and the Holy Spirit. They are an inseparable one. The Holy Spirit is the gift from the Father. However, like any gift, you can have the package, but until you open it, you can't access the gift.

So what did Jesus command His followers to do to receive the Holy Spirit? Wait expectantly, actively engage in waiting and become ready (Acts 1:1-4). It's rather like calling a friend and asking them to come see you. A true friend will not disappoint you.

The Holy Spirit is the closest, and truest friend you will ever have. So you invite and then actively wait. The Holy Spirit resides in every Christian. This prayer only opens the door to a relationship to the part of the Godhead that imparts power and knowledge. Then the believer may successfully live the Christian experience.

You could also ask someone who already has had this experience to lay hands on you and impart the Holy Spirit. You can say the following prayer yourself.

> Jesus,
>
> I ask you to baptize me in your Holy Spirit and with fire! I invite the Holy Spirit to be my friend, my teacher and my guide.
>
> Amen

What should you expect when you receive prayer? The first sign is speaking in tongues. Speaking in tongues comes from opening your mouth and making an effort to produce sounds. As you do this the Holy Spirit will take over and give confirmation with the experience of a brand, new language. It takes an effort and a yielding of your tongue as an act of faith. It takes an action as in trying to make sounds. The Holy Spirit will confirm.

Now, whenever you have a prayer you do not know how to pray, you can pray in tongues and the Holy Spirit will hear what is coming from your heart. Praying in tongues edifies and builds up the believer. It is a time of uttering mysteries to God (I Corinthians 14:4).

Not only will you pray with power, you will also experience a sudden opening of your spiritual eyes. You will discern with more clarity the Kingdom of God and the kingdom of darkness. Understanding in these areas will increase rapidly and dramatically.

Your emotions will respond to your decision. You will experience a great flood of emotions anywhere from overwhelming joy to a sense of great peace. Your simple act of faith opens a whole new dimension of power and relationship. t!

WHO IS THE HOLY SPIRIT?

The Holy Spirit is the third person of the Trinity. We can converse with Him and have a relationship with Him just as we have relationship and converse with God the Father or Jesus. He is ever the complete gentleman and will not push Himself onto anyone. He has a sense of humor. He is the teacher (John 16:12), the guide to all truth, our counselor (John 14:26, 16:17), the gift the Father God promised to send (Acts 1:4). He sanctifies the believer (2 Thessalonians 2;13), makes Jesus known to us (John 16:15), testifies of Jesus and helps us with our weaknesses (Romans 8:16, Romans 8:22). He can be grieved (Ephesians 4:30).

He comes to reveal Jesus. The Holy Spirit is revelation knowledge. It is through the Holy Spirit that revelation comes in both the Old Testament and the New Testaments.

In the Old Testament, revelation came through those who had the anointing of the Holy Spirit: king, priest or prophet. In the New Testament it is through that same anointing the revelation of God comes ; however, now all anointing is now available to all Christians. God demonstrates and foreshadows how the anointing works in the Old Testament so we will know how the anointing will work in the New Testament.

Know you can walk away from friendship with the Holy Spirit. The Holy Spirit offers such a precious and personal relationship with God, that if we turn away from His gift it grieves the Holy Spirit. If we grieve the Holy Spirit we need to ask forgiveness to restore relationship.

Christian character is produced by the indwelling of the Holy Spirit not by discipline or law. The indwelling Holy Spirit produces the following nine virtues in the life of a Christian: love, joy, peace, patience, kindness, goodness, gentleness, faithfulness and self-control (Galatians 5:22 Footnotes). Nine is the number for the Holy Spirit.

WORSHIP IN THE SPIRIT

God is a spirit and those who worship Him must worship Him in spirit and in truth. God has made man as body, soul and spirit. Man is a spirit being housed in a body that has a soul. The body becomes the temple of the Holy Spirit (I Corinthians 6:16, 6:19 3:16).The soul of man is his mind, will and emotions.

Man is a spirit being and has a need to worship. If man does not worship God, man will find something else to worship. With the gift of tongues man can present to God perfect worship, praise, intercession and prayers that will fulfill man body, soul and spirit.

There are two categories of speaking in tongues. One is for personal edification and intercession and the other is to prophesy in the Church. If tongues are spoken as a message of prophecy to the Church, the message needs to be interpreted (Corinthians 14:1-5).

GIFTS OF THE HOLY SPIRIT

The Holy Spirit not only has the nine fruits of the Spirit that He is producing in the Christian, He has nine gifts that He shares with His friends. He gives these gifts to the Christian community for the common good. He sovereignly decides which gift or gifts each believer should have. The gifts are: wisdom, knowledge, faith, gifts of healing, miraculous powers, prophecy, the ability to distinguish between spirits, speaking in tongues, and interpretation of tongues (I Corinthians 12:1-11 footnote).

1.   **Message of Wisdom**
     Gift that meets the need of the Christian community when wisdom is needed to make a decision.

2.   **Gift of Knowledge**
     Gift that meets the need of the Christian community when knowledge is required to make decisions, understanding is required to know where to pray, or information from the Holy Spirit is needed to know when and where God is moving or He is healing.

3.   **Faith**
     This kind of faith is not saving faith but extra faith to meet a specific need.

4.   **The Gifts of Healing**
     The various ways God imparts healing: It can be from laying on of hands, anointing with oil, deliverance, faith, words of knowledge, through inner healing, handkerchiefs that have been prayed over. Healing can come quickly or over a period of time.

5.   **Miraculous Powers**
     An action that is not explained by natural means. An act of God intended to evidence His power and authority.

6.   **Prophecy**
     A communication of the mind of God imparted to the believer by the Holy Spirit. It is a predictor or the indication of God's will in a given situation.

7.   **Distinguishing between Spirits**
     A necessary gift to distinguish the true Spirit from the false spirit.

8. **Different kinds of Tongues**
   The ability to speak in diverse languages, earthly or heavenly, when the Holy Spirit prompts one to do so. And the ability to pray in a private prayer language.
9. **Interpretation of Tongues**
   The ability to interpret a message in tongues so that hearers can understand.

The Holy Spirit not only gives His friends gifts, He teaches them how to use them. These gifts are for believers for the winning of the battle. The Holy Spirit knows how to win the battle and the war. We just ask and He reveals creative ways. In the Old Testament, wars were won in unusual ways. At the battle of Jericho the Israelites just marched and blew trumpets and the walls came tumbling down (Joshua 5:13-6:20).

Battles were sometimes fought as regular military offenses, but they were always under the direction of the Holy Spirit. As long as God's people obeyed, they won. When they were disobedient, they lost.

As we are obedient and follow the voice of the Holy Spirit, we can be guaranteed that the battle will be won; the ground will be taken. After all, warfare is all about who owns the land.

The first land we need to possess is our own land, our own family, our own home. This text is about the taking of spiritual land. It is the Training Manual for would-be land owners.

<u>Training Manual for Land Ownership</u>

2
Know the Enemy

If you are working or dabbling in enemy territory you need to change territories. If you are associating only with those who are in spiritual captivity you will be seeing the negative, hearing the negative and being deceived. You will lose your vision and dreams and become a captive yourself. Familiar and evil spirits have the right to lurk where sin is embraced. Watch where your feet walk, who you call friends, what your mind receives as truth, where you spend your time and where you choose to hang out. Stand with other believers and reach out to the lost but do not let the lost direct or infect your life.

Keep the vision clear! We are on the side that wins! Know God's angels watch over the Christian family, and the power of two-thirds of the heavenly hosts are on the side of the believer! Angelic functions are outlined in the text, *The Kingdom.*

Recognize the enemy! We war not against flesh and blood but against rulers, principalities and powers in high places The battle is not against other people, our spouses, other Christians, bosses, teachers or politicians. They are not the enemy!

Our struggle is not against flesh and blood but against the rulers, against the authorities, against powers of this dark world, against the spiritual forces of evil in heavenly realms. (Ephesians 6:12).

The enemy is the unseen forces of darkness, Satan and his fallen troop of demonic spirits, the fallen angels.

Fallen angels are the forces of evil. They can not create anything new, not even an organization. Therefore, they have to perform using the organization God created. They simply twist, pervert and corrupt existing Godly organization.

Their leader is the fallen angel, Satan. His original name was, Son of the Morning Star. He is also known as, Lucifer, the Prince of Darkness, the Lord of the Flies, the king of the Abyss. He can appear as an angel of light. His evil intent is to possess men's souls. His light is only a false light that tricks people into captivity and total darkness. He is the father of nothing but lies.

He presents sin as great fun. He lays out an easy path to hell. We know sin can be fun for a season. However, Satan exacts a hefty price for anyone dabbling in his territory. That price comes wrapped in oppression and captivity. He offers a free, one-way ticket to hell for the unwary. He offers power in return for bondage, power in return, the ownership of our souls.

What he does not have is the power to be omnipresent or to be all-knowing. His jurisdiction, authority and time are limited. He is a defeated foe who runs around like a roaring lion seeking foolish souls he may destroy. Because he was defeated by the death and resurrection of Jesus, we can have the authority over him and can reclaim the authority lost at the garden of Eden. At the fall, Adam relinquished the reign of the earthly realm. Through abdication Satan became the prince of this world. He holds title in the kingdom of the air (Ephesians 2: 2). We know his empty promises are always full of hot air.

Even though we can regain ground, there will always be evil until the end of time when God throws Satan, the deceiver, into the fires of hell forever! Until then, Satan will always ply his trade and his lies. He yearns to be the very center of attention. He yearns to be worshiped. Constant attention or focus on him and his power gives him the worship he craves. He produces false revelation and makes war with the saints.

Satan can exert a force over an area (territory) because of sin that has been invited (committed) in that area over a long period of time.

Some people engage in seeking a spirit guide. A spirit guide is the antithesis of the Holy Spirit. It is an evil spirit disguised to woo the foolish into deception. A spirit guide can appear as an angel of light. However, if it is not in total agreement with the Scripture, does not acknowledge that Jesus Christ came in the flesh, Jesus as the only way to God the Father and will not worship Jesus, it is not the Holy Spirit and is not to be received.

If you ask for the Holy Spirit from God the Father you will not receive an evil spirit. If you are under deception you need to repent and command, in the Name of Jesus, the deceptive spirit to leave through the door it entered. Then close that door! Finally, invite the Holy Spirit in to come and fill the vacated space. You can ask others to help pray.

In studying how the enemy works we cannot always blame everything on him. We often give him way too much credit. As believers we still have to overcome the desires of our flesh and choices of our free will. Free will is discussed in *The Kingdom - Christian Primary I.*

The Functions of the Fallen Angels

1. To offer glory and worship to Satan

2. To produce false revelations

3. To war with the Saints of God

4. To bind, blind and hinder Christians

5. To desecrate and hinder the Gospel

6. To possess men

A constant attention or focus on Satan gives him the worship he desires. As Christians he is not to be our focus. Rather it is to be our focus that in each area of deliverance the Name of Jesus is higher above every spirit in this world and in the next. Satan should not be our constant topic of conversation. It is the Name of Jesus we are to lift up.

It is the devil's delight to drag everyone he can into his hell. Hell is a place prepared for the fallen angels and Satan, not for people. People choose to go there by not accepting the free gift of salvation. It is a place of suffering and being forever separated from the goodness of God.

It is not the fun place portrayed in cartoons. It is a place of torment (Luke16:23) and a place of fire (Matthew 5:22, 18:9) It is Satan's final resting place of doom. It is a place of everlasting torment.

And the devil who deceived them was thrown into the lake of burning sulfur where the beast and the false prophet had been thrown.   They will be tormented day and night for ever and ever (Revelation 20:10).

If anyone's name is not found in the Book of Life he is thrown into the lake of fire (Revelation 20:15).

FORBIDDEN PRACTICES: OCCULT AND CULT

Satanic appointments are Satanists, witches, mediums etc. His ways are hidden, mystical, psychic, secret and controlling. These are practices that are strictly forbidden for Christians to be involved in or with.

God says, "I am against your magic charms where you ensnare people like birds" (Ezekiel 12:20).

The Bible consistently avoids explicit descriptions of occult practices, however the Bible does list exact practices God considers forbidden.

When you enter the land the Lord your God is giving you do not learn to imitate the detestable ways of the nations there. Let no one be found among you who sacrifices his sons or daughters in the fire, who practices divination or sorcery, interprets omens, who engages in witchcraft, or cast spells or who is a medium or spiritist or who consults with the dead (Deuteronomy 18:9-12).

King Saul is a great example and warning to us here. He set up a monument in his own honor, lied to the prophet Samuel, and shifted the blame to his men for not following the Word of God given to him by the prophet.

Saul lost the physical Kingdom he was ruling as he looked to self-worship, disobeying the Word of the Lord and passing the blame - rebellion (the sin of witchcraft). He was rejected by God as king (I Samuel 15:12-23)..

Later after Samuel's death we find Saul so desperate that he consults the Witch of Endor to conjure up the Prophet Samuel (Samuel:28. 7-11). The next day Saul dies.

If we don't swallow the lie of witchcraft /rebellion another ploy of the enemy is to get us involved with what might on the surface seem a positive choice - a cult. Occult activities are fairly obvious. Cults are usually more difficult to recognize as on the surface and what you see is usually their marketplace face. However, hidden behind the surface, is treacherous deception.

A cult is a religious organization such as Jehovah's Witnesses, Mormonism or Christian Scientist. It is an organization that closely impersonates and parallels truth to delude the uneducated, unwary and needy. Some cults are not as close to Christianity but rather have an oriental base.

Satan uses man's natural and spiritual desire to worship and sets up areas of false worship to entrap him. The safest area is to know basic Christian doctrine and have a through background in Scripture. *The Kingdom - Christian Primary I* is an excellent resource of information for basic Christian doctrine, and information on participating in the Christian experience.

Training Manual for Land Ownership

3
Prepare for Battle

Deliverance is not a matter of knowing formulas but rather of knowing God and living in personal relationship with His Holy Spirit. This book gives you information. The Holy Spirit offers revelation for application. If you pray every word in this text in a day, that would not necessarily bring deliverance. There are principles to learn and practice. Deliverance needs to be under the leading, direction and prompting of the Holy Spirit. Speaking one word under the direction of the Holy Spirit is better than speaking thousands of words through your own energies.

Knowledge of God is the beginning of wisdom. However, seeking after knowledge is wrong if that knowledge is elevated above a relationship with Jesus. We need the relationship in order to know how to pray. And most importantly, we cannot be dependent on others for our relationship with God or we will remain weak. God is a jealous God and He desires an intimate relationship with each of us.

As we are dependent upon Him, God provides the position and the tools to win the battle. He sets the Kingdom tone of warfare through the following proclamation.

The weapons we fight with are not the weapons of the world. On the contrary, they have divine power to demolish strongholds. We demolish arguments and every pretension that sets itself up against the knowledge of God and we take captive every thought to make it obedient to Christ (II Corinthians 10:12).

DIFFERENT APPROACHES

Different people can embrace different approaches and reach the same goal. That does not make one approach wrong and the other right. There are different perspectives, different personalities, different church backgrounds, different levels of authority and different mandates from God. The goal is the same, however, and each can be looking or working at the problem from a different perspective, as long as that perspective is in complete agreement with Scripture.

There is a story of four blind monkeys who had found an elephant. One held a foot, another the trunk, another the tail and another the ear. They had all found an elephant. However each had their own interpretation of truth. Saint Paul said, "I see through a glass darkly" So do we! Have patience with yourself and with others (Ephesians 4:1-16).

We are in a war, but a war fought not with the ways of humankind. We must know the principles and how to fight. If we fight in a traditional way we may win a battle but lose the war.

We keep the goal in mind: growing together in a relationship with Jesus, knowing Him, loving Him and walking in His Kingdom ways. The goal cannot be deliverance. A constant or unnecessary attention on the enemy gives him the attention and worship. Our goal is to worship Jesus!

Rejoice not that demons flee from you but that your names are written in the Lamb's Book of Life (Luke 10:20).

MISTAKES

Mistakes are a part of the learning process. We need to apply wisdom and try to avoid mistakes but admit them when they happen. You did not learn to write your alphabet by making every letter perfect the first time. Mistakes are a part of the process.

Look and listen for confirmation in direction. Read the Word and develop a relationship with God, the Holy Spirit. Listen for His voice. As you listen you will begin to recognize His leading. It is always a voice deep inside. A voice that is not our own. It is a calm urging, prompting, knowing and an assurance to go ahead or it is a caution to stop.

There are consequences to making mistakes. It is wise in areas where the risk is great to have a lot of input and prayer from others. Continue to move in a direction you think is right but be prepared to change directions if the door closes.

Allow others to edit unneeded ideas and listen with discernment. Have a learner's attitude. Be careful that you do not demand perfectionism for yourself or for others.

Allow patience for the mistakes of others, encourage them and pray wisdom and blessing for them. Realize they are learners just like you.

TAKE A STAND

Is God calling you to pray, speak out or take a stand? Be willing to redirect your effort or make adjustments in the journey. With our human minds we can reason God's final outcome for our direction while God had another purpose entirely. Be actively listening.

There are times you pray with a partner, especially when someone needs serious help. One person may pray aloud while the another intercedes. Jesus dispatched His disciples two-by-two for: *One can chase a thousand, two can put ten thousand to flight (Deuteronomy 32:30).*

. It is not wise to leave an opening for the enemy. An area

to avoid being alone where a man is praying for a woman or a woman is praying for a man. The enemy can use innocent situations. Do not assume you can walk easily where others fell. The enemy likes to set traps. He allows you to beome over-confident in your own abilities and then he makes his move.

Concerning personalities, there are Christians and non-Christians alike who will say things to you in private and even threaten and humiliate you in an attempt to control you, but show a completely different face to the public. It becomes a matter of your word against theirs on what they said and who they really are.

If this person is in a position of respect in a particular community they often get away with their private behavior. Do not be caught in the web of counseling or talking alone with this kind of manipulator.

Some people will flatter you in order to use you. Listen carefully. Discern what people are really saying. A woman with an evil spirit followed Saint Paul. She flattered him but in reality she was using Him and His anointing.

If someone is speaking against you personally and they are under the influence of an evil spirit, you can bind that evil spirit and command it to stop just as Saint Paul did.

In situations where you see a public area you need to stand against or pray against listen for the still, small voice of God. Is He calling you to pray or is this simply a distraction used by the enemy to keep you too busy to fulfill your true calling?

Are you full of prayers like the Pharisee who likes his own voice? Whose works are you doing anyway? Do you pray out of love? Are you using the authority God has given you? Adequately covering yourself from the attacks of the enemy? Coming with clean heart and standing free of unforgiveness and judgment? Do you know the Word of God? Then continue watching and listening for the discernment of the Holy Spirit.

As you begin the battle be sure you dress for the occasion for the Kingdom of Heaven is taken by violence and the violent take it by force. The violence is not against other people but towards the taking of the heavenly realm and entering into the promises and the rest of God's Kingdom.

This type of violence includes active personal commitment and participation: forgiving, choosing to love, discipline, healing, faith, knowing the Word of God, pulling down strongholds, and listening. The battle is not against flesh and blood but against powers, principalities and rulers in high places.

Because the battle is not against flesh and blood lay down your own weapons of warfare towards each other. Sometimes with a conscious knowledge, sometimes unknowingly, we are armed to the teeth to battle against other denominations, colors, people or our spouses.

If we could see ourselves in the spirit we might see something like this: Sword grasped tightly between the teeth, a belt of hand grenades slung over our shoulders, our hands gripping a rifle, (our bible) equipped with a silencer and night scope, and our combat boots firmly planted for confrontation or any challenge. Ask the Spirit to reveal any areas you need to lay down your weapons towards others so that you might begin the battle against the real enemy. Take a few moments to meditate.

> Holy Spirit, I ask your forgiveness that I have fought against_____my brothers and sisters in Christ, I ask forgiveness that I have set a battle against my spouse_____ , my family_____.
> I lay down my weapons of warfare and destruction.

THE SUIT OF LIGHT

Now to become armed and dangerous. It begins with proper dress in a supernatural "light" suit called the armor of God.

What is the armor of God? It's like an invisible, spiritual suit or protective covering so that we may battle invisible forces of the enemy. The enemy is not the visible husband, wife, child, boss, other Christians or non-believers although it can look as if they are the enemy. Dealing with the battle using human resources is impossible. Know whom you battle and battle with spiritual weapons.

> *Therefore put on the full armor of God so that when the day of evil comes you may be able to stand your ground. (Eph 6:11-13)*

Lord, I put on the full armor of God, *the belt of truth buckled around my waist, with the breastplate of righteousness in place and with my feet fitted with the readiness that comes from the Gospel of peace. I take up the shield of faith with which I can extinguish all the flaming arrows of the evil one. I place the helmet of Salvation upon my head and wield the sword of the Spirit which is the Word of God. I pray in the Spirit (tongues) on all occasions (Ephesians 6:14-18).* Holy Spirit, I now set aside my own wisdom and actively seek and ask for your wisdom. I invite you to speak through me.

The armour is really a "light" suit. It is a light suit in that it is very light in weight and it is a light suit in that is actually putting on the Glory of Jesus. This light of Jesus is revealed in each part of the armour.

The *Girdle of Truth*, is the light we walk under. It surrounds our inner parts with the light of God's truth.The *Helmet of Salvation*, is red. It protects our mind from the enemy. The *Breastplate of Righteousness*, means having a right relationship with God. Our right standing with God only comes through the blood of Jesus, so the breastplate is red. The *Shoes of Peace* are blue. They enable us to walk in the way of God's peace and to be gentle with those who are weak. *The Shield of Faith* is also blue. *The Sword of the Spirit* is golden for it is the Word of God. *Praying in Tongues* expresses the perfect prayer to the Father by taking control of your most unruly member - your tongue. Our prayers go up as golden incense before the throne of God.

The armour is in the three primary colors. Literally you are putting on the Glory of God when you put on the armour. When you put on this "light" suit it reflects the Glory of God for the enemy to see. When you pray with someone else, pray the armor of

God prayer aloud as you begin your warfare.

If pressed for an immediate prayer and I don't have time to pray the above, I will plead for the blood of Jesus to cover myself and my family. The Israelites placed the blood of the lamb upon the doorposts when they were in bondage in Egypt. It marked them as God's people and protected them.

I have had several experiences where I have not applied this truth of putting on the Armor of God and found myself physically being hurt, spiritually being attacked, having less strength and feeling as if the battle would overwhelm me. Without the protection of the armor of God I open a door for evil to directly have an advantage, and I feel its' weight and gloominess.

If I have carelessly allowed myself into this kind of predicament and cannot pray myself, I will find a friend, one who knows how to use authority, and together we will pray to shove back the enemy. Praying without protection is lack of wisdom and foolishness.

As I pray I always open a door or a window. I allow a way for the spirit to leave.

REACTIONS TO PRAYER

Some reactions you might expect as a result of praying for someone are: Yawning, sneezing, coughing, a runny nose, lots of spit in the mouth.

Christians who want deliverance can have these reactions but the prayer is easy because of their acceptance. Afterwards there will be a great feeling of lightness, especially in the stomach area. Their face will appear lighter and the room will look lighter brighter. There is a feeling of lightness as if a great weight has lifted. The person who received prayer and the person who prayed can both feel these positive reactions. This is the more common experience with deliverance.

Reactions can be more severe: vomiting, rolling on the floor, resisting and fighting against those who are praying. This is the kind of deliverance we hear more about because it is so dramatic. In either case the Christian has authority.

You do not always have to be loud when praying.

Sometimes a soft voice is adequate. When you have authority you do not have to yell. Follow the leading of the Holy Spirit. If you then feel the necessity to be loud, be loud!

Above all, be balanced! Not every situation demands deliverance! People can be suffering from burn out, vitamin deficiencies, chemical imbalances due to medications or exposure to chemicals. They may need to be anointed with oil for the forgiveness of sin or they may need inner healing, they may need to simply choose to change their behavior, they may need to be disciplined.

Training Manual for Land Ownership

4
Tools of Warfare

One of the greatest instruments of warfare you will need is discernment. Discernment means not depending upon your own knowledge or wisdom but rather actively listen to directions from the Holy Spirit. He is your guide to all truth.

You listen allowing Scripture or pictures the Holy Spirit may give to assist in the prayer. The Holy Spirit will not only direct but He will confirm as He directs. Confirmation is part of the direction. This way of prayer takes time and errors can occur as you learn how to share visions and discern between your own ways and the ways of the Holy Spirit.

Share humbly as you are learning. You can say, "I believe I see," instead of "God told me or "Thus sayeth the Lord." Allow the person you are praying for to judge the vision. If it is from God you do not need to defend it.

Another tactic the enemy (through the world) uses is called subliminal subjection. Subliminal subjection is when things are hitting us a level that our eye sees so quickly we do not even know it was there but our mind picks up the picture or thought and stores it or perhaps reacts to it.

This is used in advertisements where there are hidden pictures. You may be looking at a man guzzling beer. The art work has hidden pictures to stir your desires. Some of these images can be very pornographic. Just be aware the objective of the world is to make money. They will do what ever it takes and be as deceptive as they can get away with in order to have that marketing (sales) edge. Know that the world is out to make money and is not interested in your best interests, although the appeal may sound as if they are.

MUSIC, PRAISE, WORSHIP AND LAUGHTER

In the Old Testament, singers and those playing on instruments, were sent out into battle before the army of Israel (2 Chronicles 20). This was an unusual way to fight a physical battle but one of the ways given as an example of how to win a war. If you are a musician, God intends for you to be in front of the warriors, praising and singing.

Music has power over the soul. Music passes the mind and moves uncensored into the soul. It can have a positive or negative affect on the soul as well as the air.

By using music, the singers not only encouraged the souls of those around them, they also dethroned the prince of the air and took the air space for God. Their faith surrounded them as they prepared for battle. No one could stand against them. The psalmist commands, "Praise the Lord! Come into His presence with praise and thanksgiving."

It is through praise, an attitude of gratitude, that we enter God's presence. Praise unleashes the supernatural and routs the enemy. Praise lifts the darkness and produces miraculous changes.

God does not expect Christians to praise evil but praise because God is in control. Part of praising is dancing, singing and laughter. Old Testament musicians sang and danced before their army as it moved into battle.

Worship is the highest form of praise. Worship becomes an intimate experience between God and the believer. When Christians worship, they join with the angels and all the saints in heaven to proclaim: "Our God reigns! "

Laughter is an instrument of healing and laughter can be an instrument of war. We can laugh at the enemy. We can join with God and laugh. God is a God of laughter.

He who sits in the heavens laughs at the enemy(Psalm 2).

SCRIPTURE

In face-to-face confrontation with the devil in the desert, Jesus quoted Scripture to refute his offers. Scripture is the base, the foundation for defeating the enemy. We can be taken advantage of, fall into a trap of the enemy, if we do not know God and His Word. Get discernment from the Holy Spirit but know the Scriptures!

My people are destroyed because of lack of knowledge (Hosea 4:1).

The fear of the Lord is the beginning of knowledge but fools despise wisdom and discipline (Proverb1:7).

Not only do we need to know the Word, we also need to be educated. The following chapter explores a step-by-step pattern for prayer. Why do we have to go into such detail to recognize each evil spirit and all areas that are part of its boundaries?

When Jesus spoke to a spirit, He knew the sum total of who and what he was addressing. That gave Him authority! We need to know, recognize and have authority over the sum total of whom we are addressing and then, we too, will have authority with just a word.

Spirits can work in an individual effort or they can work as a group. When dealing with a group, we must address all that goes into that group in order to be effective.

The "Good News" is that groups are easily predictable as we follow the color pattern. As we stand against these groups we will feel the power of the darkness. The darkness will only become worse if not addressed. We have no choice but to address the battle or grow more into bondage. Addressing the battle will cause us to grow in strength. Our position is one of authority. The battle is already won! The victory is ours! The enemy is defeated at the Cross! It is simply a matter of walking out that victory.

Is this the only pattern for deliverance? Absolutely not! The Holy Spirit can give instant discernment and direction and you need not know this pattern at all. This pattern only helps you in your understanding the relationship between spirits.

THE SECRET CODE - THE COLOR STAR

The secret code is the color star. It is a color wheel that locates the strongmen and reveals their nature and intent. Through negative color chart you can begin to recognize how the spirits relate and work together. In this text we study how negative color reveals the language of the enemy as well as how negative color reveals relationships between spirits.

The color star locates each evil spirit's function. You can see how it relates to other spirits and how to pray and break its power using the graph. Color defines the battle and lays out the strategy and pattern for winning the war. The color chart is simply a color wheel used as a visual aid to explain relationships. For example, if you are considering the negative color green, you can know that the Spirit of Jealousy (green) is then made up of yellow and blue and a compliment to red. The chart reveals relationship. Color theory, the color wheel, primaries and secondarys are explained in *The Glory - Christian Primary II.*

The color star will also reveal the voice you hear with each spirit and the number (revealing relationship). Understanding the voice you hear and the negative number helps identify the language that spirit speaks. The sound of negative voice and the meanings of negative numbers is also covered in *The Glory -Christian Primary II.*

When you pray you need to differentiate between oppression and possession. Oppression means to weigh heavily upon and distress mentally or physically. Possession means to be taken over by (ownership). Evil spirits can only oppress Christians. Non-Christians can be possessed. You are still dealing with the same evil but how fully it can afflict or control you is dependent on being Christian or non-Christian.

THE COLOR STAR

The Color Star is a color wheel to locate colors. It is used as the base to identify language and relationship. In the Glory you learned how Jesus speaks the Kingdom positive language of six: 6 colors, 6 voices and 6 numbers. The enemy cannot create a new language so he also speaks a language of six. Of course he speaks negative color, voice and number.

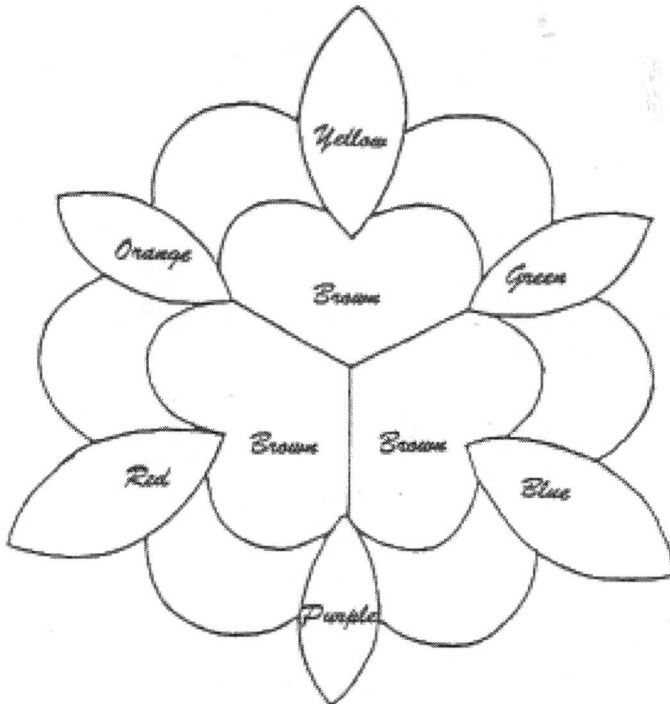

Training Manual for Land Ownership

5
Take the Land

In *The Glory - Christian Primary II* you learned of the Language of Light that God speaks and the language of lies that the enemy speaks. Color was revealed as a vehicle through which you could discern the differences in the languages. In *The Power- Christian Primary III* you will be viewing negative color. Through the color stars it will be overlaid for you to view the negative voice you will hear and the negative number as you just study the language of darkness..

All colors that follow are negative colors. Individual spirits are negative. Fuller descriptions of negative colors, voices and numbers can be found in *The Glory - Christian Primary II.*

We know that the pattern is God's. The deception is from the enemy. What follows is only the negative applications of color for the language we hear from the enemy will be under the light of the lie as presented In *The Glory* pages 10-14.

Each primary color will have two voices under each heading. Each secondary color has one.

NAMES OF EVIL SPIRITS

There are spirits named in the Bible other than those mentioned. Those mentioned in the Bible with other names I believe are only some of the same spirits addressed with a compatible name. Look at the negative fruit that the spirit produces. You can recognize the evil spirit by the fruit it yields, the voice it speaks with and the bondage it offers.

The first six are individual spirits. The last three are listed as groups. The total is nine. The enemy can only have nine as nine is the number of the Holy Spirit . The devil cannot produce a new pattern, he can only use the pattern established by God.

Now there can be many spirits under each heading of a head spirit. This text does not presume to list everything. It lists only the pattern and some examples. It is a study text that you can add to as you learn more. First the evil spirits will be listed on a line and then placed on graphs.

0-9. The Lying Spirit includes religious spirits
    All evil spirits are lying spirits. They
    all function under the light of the lie ~ white.

1. A Proud and Haughty Spirit and a Spirit of Infirmity ~ Yellow

2. The Spirit of Rebellion and a Spirit of Perversion ~ Red

3   The Spirit of Fear and a Spirit of Depression ~ Blue

3. The Spirit of the Deaf and Dumb ~ Orange

4. The Spirit of Jealousy ~ Green

5. The Spirit of Whoredom ~ Purple

6.   The Spirit of Bondage ~ Brown

0-9   The Spirit of the anti-christ . All evil spirits are spirits that come against Jesus. All evil spirits are anti-christ spirits.

NAME ABOVE ALL NAMES

As well as being a book of learning about the fruits and gifts of the Holy Spirit, this is a text book on deliverance. And so there are graphs for the nine evil spirits. Know that demonic forces have names and we can call them out by their names.

However there is a name above all names and that name is the Name of Jesus. He is the King of Kings and the Lord of Lords and at His Name every knee must bow and every tongue confess that He is Lord. That every knee must bow includes the knees of demonic spirits!

Therefore God exalted Him (Jesus) to the highest place and gave Him the name that is above every name, that at the Name of Jesus every knee should bow, in heaven and on earth and under the earth, and every tongue confess that Jesus Christ is Lord to the Glory of God the Father (Philippians 2:9-11).

As you read through the following you will see the demonic spirits represented on color wheel graphs. Above and over the top of each is the Name of Jesus for the Name of Jesus is exalted above every name. His name is higher and is depicted as higher.

Know that you have the authority over every demonic spirit because of Jesus. Jesus has been raised up to high place of spiritual authority and He has raised up the believer to sit beside Him. Jesus offers to believers the power that He has. It is a great power. That's the kind of power that raises the dead.

For this reason, ever since I heard about your faith in the Lord Jesus and your love for all the saints, I have not stopped giving thanks for you remembering you in my prayers. I keep asking that the God of our Lord Jesus Christ, the glorious Father, may give you the spirit of wisdom and revelation so that you may know Him better.

I pray also that the eyes of your heart may be enlightened in order that you may know hope to which He has called you, the riches of His glorious inheritance in the saints, and the incomparably great power for us who believe.

That power is like the working of His mighty strength, which He exerted in Christ when He raised Him from the dead and seated Him at His right hand in heavenly realms far above all rule and authority, power and dominion and every title that can be given not only in the present age but also in the one to come (Ephesians 1:17-21).

And God raised us up with Christ and seated us with Him in the heavenly realms in Christ Jesus (Ephesians 2:6).

THE LANGUAGE OF DARKNESS - A LANGUAGE OF SIX

The following pages will list the first six spirits on individual color stars. Color the portion of the color star as marked. The first six spirits are listed in numerical order. The color, voice and number are notated on the middle right side of the page. The sets of seven through nine reveal how spirits work in a group. They are not new, but rather, combinations of one through six.

This is the same pattern of language you learned in the book *The Glory*. Only in *The Glory* the primary focus was on God's language of light (color), voice and number. Here the focus is entirely the language of the enemy and his negative language of six colors, six voices and six numbers. He can only function and speak in the pattern God created. So he uses the language pattern God created, only he perverts it. Know that color is the light Satan works under, voice is the name he goes by and number speaks of relationship.

As you color the following negative color stars you may want to look back at how you placed the colors, voices and numbers around the color star when you studied the language of God. The following color stars will have colors, voices and numbers in the same place, however, they will all be negatives.

The color star used in this study is from, COLOR, A Complete Guide for Artists, by Ralph Fabri, Watson-Guptill Publications And used with permission.

<u>JESUS</u> THE LIGHT OF THE WORLD
THE WAY, THE TRUTH, THE LIFE
The Lying Spirit

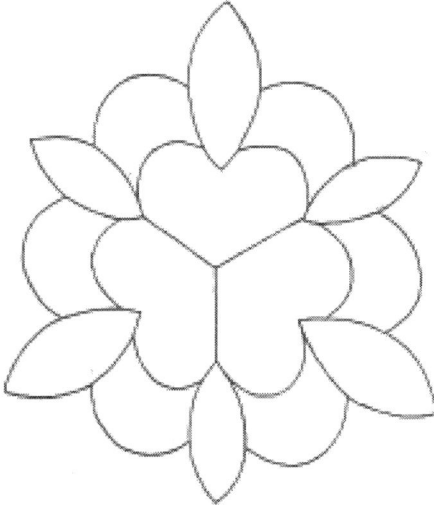

**COLOR - White/Light
VOICE - The Father
  of Lies
NUMBERS 0 - 9**

The Voice, The Manifestation, The Fruit
<u>2 Chronicles 18:20-22</u>

LIes	**Sleepiness in spiritual issues**
Exaggerations	**Complacency**
Falsehoods	
Being Religious	
Strong Delusions	

All spirits in this study are lying spirits - spirits of error. The lie is the light through which you enter the kingdom of lies and darkness. Lying is the native language of Satan.

The Religious Spirit causes a thick fog-like blanket that shuts down the anointing. A religious spirit grieves the spirit. Command it to lift. The air will appear clear and crisp. Never be underneath or controlled by a person with a religious spirit! Take authority! Take authority over sleepiness and complacency.

JESUS LION OF THE TRIBE OF JUDAH
THE KING OF KINGS

The Haughty Spirit
The Spirit of Infirmity

COLOR - Yellow
VOICE - Pride/
Bitterness/ Sickness
NUMBER - 1

The Voice, The Manifestation, The Fruit

Haughty Spirit Proverbs 16:18-19   Spirit of Infirmity Luke 13:11-12

Pride/Critical Spirit	**Lingering Disorders**
Bitterness/control	**Back Problems**
Mocking, Scorn	**Frailty**
Haughty	**Self-Pity**
Self-Worship	**Arthritis/Cancer**
Bragging, Boastful	**Physical Disease**
Worship of Idols	**Allergies**
Egotistical/Controlling	**Self-loathing**

Gluttony/Alcoholism (when it is a control issue)
Vanity/self-centered/Gossip
Critical Tongue/Mocking Laughter
Humanism/Atheism

A Proud and Haughty Spirit can reveal itself through a foul smell, a mocking attitude, bitterness or self-pity.

<u>JESUS</u> THE LAMB THAT WAS SLAIN
OUR HIGH PRIEST

<u>Spirit of Perversion</u>
<u>Witchcraft/Rebellion</u>

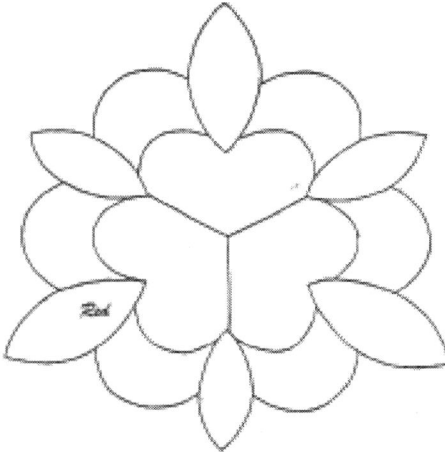

COLOR - Red
VOICE - Rebellion,
Wltchcraft,
perversion
NUMBER 2

The Voice, The Manifestation, The Fruit

<u>The Spirit of Peversion</u>	<u>Spirit of Witchcraft/Familiar Spirit</u>
Isaiah 19:14 Romans 1:28	1 Samuel 28:7-8 Acts 16:16-18
	Deuteronomy 18:12 Micah 5:12

Division	**Witchcraft**
Lust	**Rebellion**
Abortion	**Consulting the dead**
Pornography	**Fortune Tellers**
Incest	**White Witchcraft**
Homosexuality	**Clairvoyant/telepathic**
Child Abuse	**Astrology**
Beastiality	**Conjure/Divine/levitate**
Perverse Mind	**Black Magic**
To pervert the Gospel	**Family Familiar**
Pagan	**Enchanter**

<u>JESUS</u> THE PRINCE OF PEACE
THE PROPHET

<u>Spirit of Heaviness</u>
<u>Spirit of Fear</u>

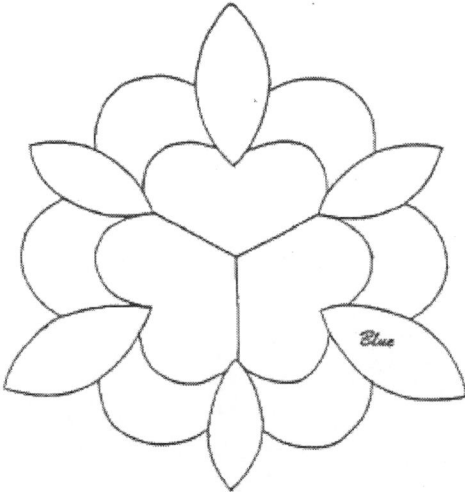

COLOR - Blue
VOICE - Fear
NUMBER - 3

The Voice, The Manifestation, The Fruit

The Spirit of Heaviness
Isaiah 61:3

Mourning
Grief
Self-Pity
Gluttony (depression)
Gloominess
Heaviness
Rejection
Loneliness
Torment

The Spirit of Fear
2 Timothy 1:7

Nervous breakdown
Torment/Phobias
Rejection
Fear of Death
Fear of Man
Unbelief
Heart Attacks
Fear
Forebodings

JESUS   THE SAVIOR OF THE WORLD
THE TRUE VINE

Spirit of Jealousy Numbers 5:14

COLOR - Green
VOICE - Jealousy
Division
NUMBER - 4

The Voice, The Manifestation, The Fruit

Spirit of Jealousy   9:17-29 Romans 1:28

Division   **Violence/abuse**
Envy   **Hoarding**
Coveting   **Revenge**
Murder   **Controlling**
Abortion   **Greed**
Lack of boundaries
Unhealthy Competition
Lack of Discipline
All physical and verbal abuse

<u>JESUS</u> THE PROPHET
THE MIGHTY COUNSELOR

<u>Deaf and Dumb</u>

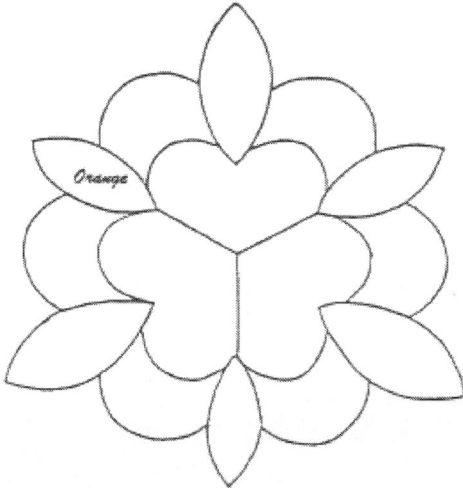

COLOR - Orange
VOICE - Suicide
NUMBER - 3

The Voice, The Manifestation, The Fruit

<u>The Deaf and Dumb</u>   Mark 9:17-29 Romans 1:28

Insanity//Lunatic	**Color Blindness**
Unteachable	**Dyslexia**
Manic	**Tongue-tied**
Nervous Breakdowns	**Inner-ear difficulties**
Suicidal tendencies/thoughts	**Anorexia/Bulmia**
Insanity/Despair	**Depression/Fear**
All cults	**Backwards Thinking**
Schizophrenia	**Contrary/anti-social**
Bipolar/Mental Illness	**Drug Addiction**

The Deaf and the Dumb Spirit steals your hope, steals your dreams and steals your future. It is the spirit very currently in the world. It makes it difficult for people to hear or receive the Gospel. The signature is suicide or suicidal thoughts.

<u>JESUS</u> THE KING OF KINGS
LORD OF LORDS

The Spirit of Whoredom

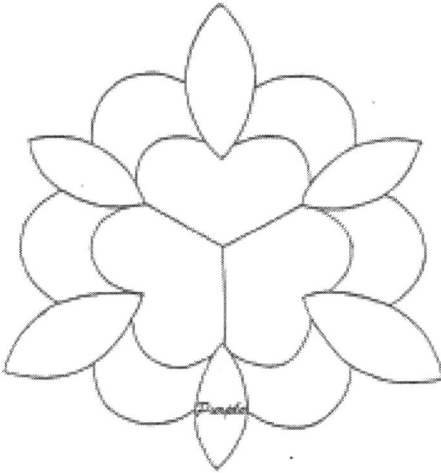

COLOR - Purple
VOICE - Prince of this World
NUMBER - 5

The Voice, The Manifestation, The Fruit

The Spirit of Whoredom   Hosea 4:12, 5:49

Worldliness	**Pride**
Scorn	**Dictatorial**
The Despotic Church	**Arrogance**
Legalism	**Self-Worship**
Love of Social Position	**Bragging**
Love of the World	**The Breach**
Controlling	**Manipulating**
Egotistical	**Controlling**
Vanity	

JESUS   THE SECOND ADAM
THE SON OF MAN

The Spirit of Bondage The Beast

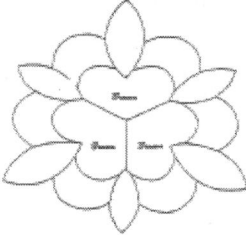

COLOR - Brown
VOICE - Captivity
NUMBER - 6

The Voice, The Manifestation, The Fruit
The Spirit of Bondage   Romans 8:16, Isaiah 61:3, 2 Timothy 1:7

Slavery in all forms   **Dirty, Unclean Spirit**
Being held captive

JESUS   THE BRIDEGROOM

The Spirit of Anti-Christ

COLOR - Black
VOICE - Darkness
NUMBERS 0 - 9

The Voice, The Manifestation, The Fruit
The Spirit of the Anti-Christ   1John:4:3   Romans 1:28
The Spirit of Death

Perverts the Word of God
Subverts Godly Authority
Persecutes the Saints
Perverts the Gospel
All that comes against Jesus and His teaching.
All evil spirits are spirits of anti-Christ as they all come against Jesus.

Note: The following graphs will be how groups come together. There are three groups: Divorce/Division, Suicide/Unteachable and total Apostasy. They are combinations of the individual spirits. In Divorce/ Division there are seven major spirits involved. In Suicide/ Unteachable there are eight major Spirits involved and in total Apostasy there are nine spirits involved.

THE SPIRITS THAT
CAUSE DIVORCE/DIVISION

The leader in this group is Jealousy. This spirit is very recognizable because it causes envy, spite, divisiveness, abuse, excessive greed. You can recognize his work as Jealousy stirs up problems to cause a separation in marriages, churches or relationships. He entices married people with an affair or thoughts of an affair. He tears apart churches, separates families, ruins friendships and can be the ruling spirit over cities. This spirit group is physically and verbally abusive.

He has been welcomed into the family due to divorce, broken relationships or opening a door to adulterous, homosexual or pornographic materials. He is the first group spirit to enter. He devastates the homeland of the soul.

Most often people who have this spirit working in their lives do not recognize the devastation as it is the only thing they are familiar with so they have nothing else to compare it to. It is a place of great familiarity - like an old shoe. Because it is all they have known it can be frightening to step out into something considered the unknown. Know that fear will attack to cause you to want to stop the battle.

There is a poverty of soul experienced daily by people under this spirit. If you see the fruit of this spirit working in your home this is the first area to start deliverance.

Jealousy could not become established until all the primaries were established. Jealousy is green. Green is a combination of blue and yellow and a compliment to primary red. All these spirits came in first and then Jealousy established the territory. So in prayer, deal with the primaries first and then topple Jealousy.

We can experience temporary peace by just ousting Jealously and be fooled into thinking we have won the battle. However if all the spirits in this mix are not considered those still in residence may invite Jealously back in. The color guide reveals a guide to prayer so that victory will be complete.

Begin with the Lying Spirit. This is the lie you have

believed, the lie that was allowed into your family by you, your parents or grandparents - the light that opened the doorway to living in darkness.

Proceed by praying over the three primaries. First blue, then red, yellow, and then you can pray green. Color becomes your guide to relationship and a guide to assist you in knowing where to pray next. It is the light on the path leading you to freedom. You can refer to the individual charts as you pray. Take your time and listen to the Holy Spirit and His guidance as you pray. Begin with blue as blue is the area for the spirit of man.

Once you sincerely recognize that you have proceeded through all areas successfully and the Holy Spirit has shown you that the Spirit of Jealousy has left, then pray brown, the Spirit of Bondage is broken. Bondage is a dirty unclean spirit and is not able to be released because of its being a combination of colors. The combination must be broken in order to release the Spirit of Bondage. Brown is just the combination of colors that worked together to form the bondage.

This kind of prayer can take a bit of time...maybe several days. Be patient. Continue to persevere until all holds are broken. The Spirit is a green dragon that has stolen your hopes of happiness. Face that green dragon and demand it leave! Take the Sword of the Spirit and turn behind you and destory the tormenting spirit that accompanies it. What you will find is a restoration you never dreamed possible.

Yes, you can pray and have instant results. Some people have that kind of authority as they are led by the Holy Spirit. This pattern simply gives you a way to proceed where you cover all the territory. For me it was a journey of several months. Of course I didn't know the pattern at that time but was learning as I went.

Know, too, that you can experience full deliverance but the spirit can come to test if you will receive it back. Just know it is now no longer living in you but making an attack from the outside. It will leave with a firm command. Its' authority at this time is broken. Walk in your new authority.

The number of spirits involved in this combination is seven.

You don't count the Lying Spirit, the Spirit of Bondage or the anti-Christ as separate spirits. They are all lying spirits, they are all spirits of bondage and they are anit-christ spirits. There are two ruling spirits in yellow: the Haughty Spirit and the Spirit of Infirmity. There are two spirits in red: the Spirit of Perversion and the Spirit of Divination (witchcraft-rebellion). There are two spirits in blue: the Spirit of Fear and Depression and the Spirit of Heaviness. One in green, Jealously. The total is seven.

When you are praying over this spirit, or any other spirit, if you are praying by yourself you can take the authority and command this spirit to leave. If you are praying with others they can take authority and command this spirit to leave. Or if others are praying for you, they may ask you to take the authority and denounce this spirit and command it to leave.

A spirit that seems to afflict those who have come from a broken home is torment. You can verbally address this torment. Take hold of the Sword of the Spirit, turn towards your back and act out slaying those spirits of torment/abanondment/abuse that have dogged their heels. Forgive. Pray for inner healing for the wounds of the soul. Speak and pray for a healing of the heart.

JESUS SAVIOR OF THE WORLD

Jealousy/Divorce

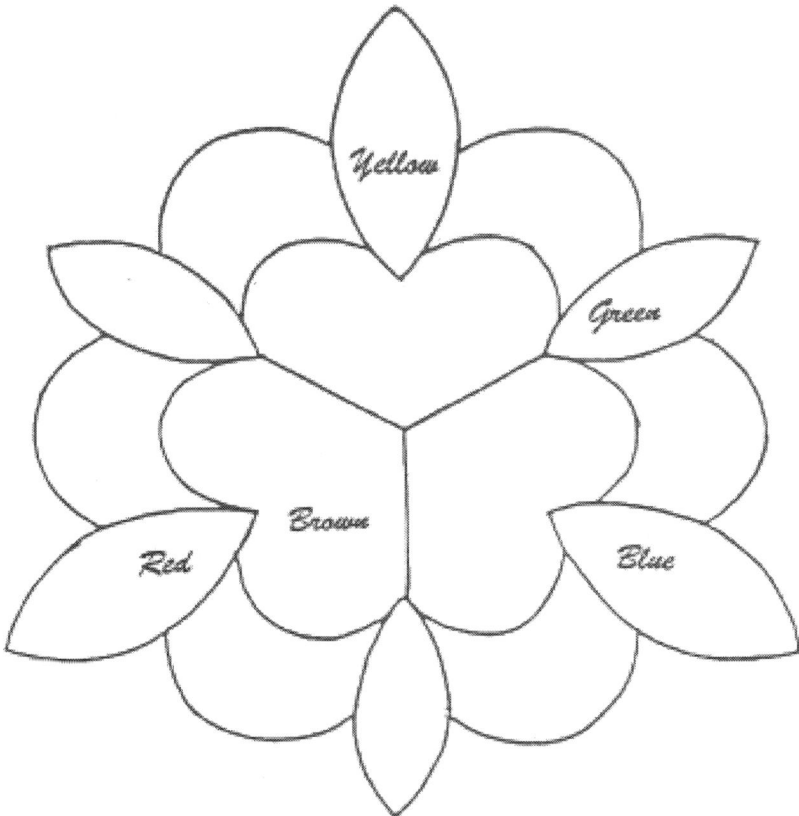

STRONGMEN 7   SPIRIT OF JEALOUSY
WHITE: Lying Spirit
YELLOW: Proud and Haughty and Spirit of Infirmity
RED: Spirit of Perversion and Witchcraft
BLUE: Spirit of Fear and Heaviness
GREEN: Spirit of Jealousy
BROWN: Spirit of Bondage
BLACK: Spirit of anti-Christ
NUMBER   7

THE SPIRITS THAT WORK TOGETHER TO CAUSE INSANITY, SUICIDE AND AN UNTEACHABLE SPIRIT

The Deaf and Dumb is the second set. It is an extremely prevalent spirit in our day and time. It is a combination that has come in after the set of Jealousy has been established. It comes in through the broken homeland. It builds upon the establishment of the group - Jealousy/Division.

When the Deaf and Dumb is active it is difficult to unravel what is really at work. So many things confront you all at once you can begin to feel crazy. That's a sure clue to the Deaf and Dumb. Feelings or thoughts of suicide are another clue, even if those thoughts are just passing thoughts.

This spirit drives people crazy, into fear, depression and nervous breakdowns causing mental or physical suicide.

The person or persons under this spirit have difficulty receiving the Word of God (hearing disorders and dyslexia).

When praying for this mix, follow the same pattern as with the last group, but also include finally all that is involved in orange - the Deaf and Dumb. Only then pray for brown, the Spirit of Bondage, to be released. Here all primaries are at work, two secondarys, and brown.

Some markers along the path to watch for: Know that the human spirit has been twisted, pray and watch that spirit become untwisted. Recognize the person is captured in a mirror image...a backwards reflection. Pray to break that backwards mirror image. If a person is dyslexic, pray the gates of Hell be broken. In dyslexia there are blockages where information cannot be received through regular nerve channels. These blockages are literally called gates. I call them gates of Hell.

What is good becomes bad to those under the influence of this mix. What is bad becomes good. The more we submit to this spirit the more demanding it becomes.

When we are dealing with a person under the influence of this spirit, submission to their will causes them only to become more demanding. They exhibit a very contrary nature. They do not maintain boundaries but are constantly stepping over personal boundaries and exhibiting anti-social behaviors. Under this spirit a perverse spirit has twisted their thinking.

I also believe that it could be a place to search for the cause of some medically defined diseases - diseases that attack memory, or memory as it relates to body functions.

One person in your family can be influenced by this most evil spirit and the Deaf and Dumb will hang around the house to pester the rest. Or it could be that this spirit is one your family inherited from your ancestors as a "Family Familiar", perhaps affecting one member more. You see the results of this spirit in schools with bright children that are unable to learn.

A real clue to the Deaf and Dumb is that it devastates the mind. This kind of devastation takes time to heal. Continue to pray for inner healing and renewal of the mind. The Deaf and Dumb is a difficult spirit to deal with. It is helpful if several people pray (as a group) to break the hold. It is helpful to pray on a regular basis. It also helps to fast.

This spirit wreaks havoc on a family or on a community.

<u>Jesus</u> The Mighty Counselor

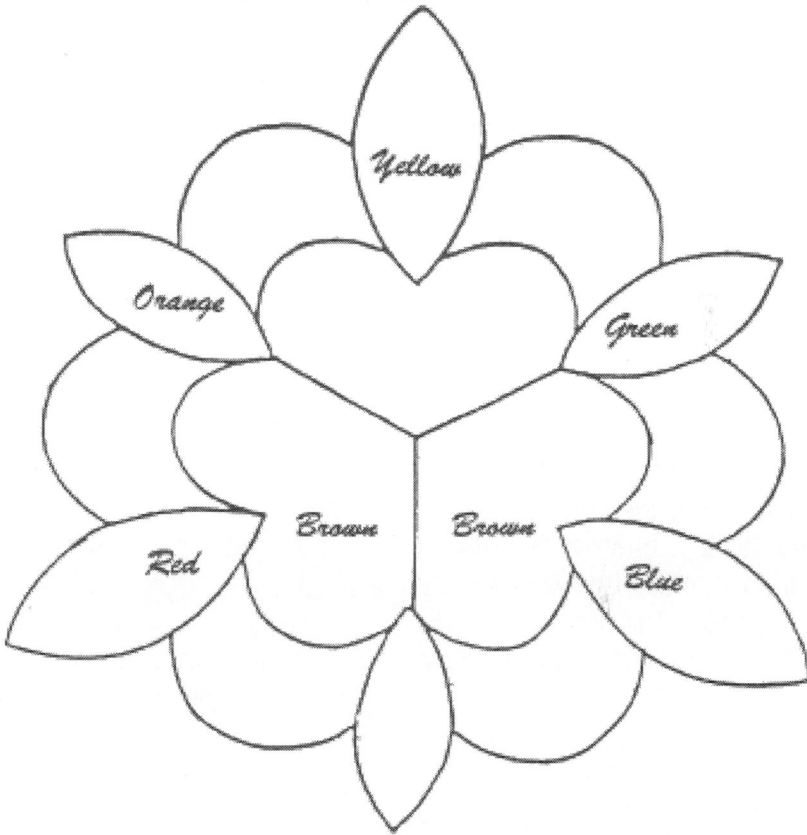

STRONGMEN 8 DEAF AND DUMB / UNTEACHABLE

WHITE: Lying Spirit
YELLOW: Proud and Haughty / Spirit of Infirmity
RED: Spirit of Perversion and Witchcraft
BLUE: Spirit of Fear and Spirit of Heaviness
GREEN: Spirit of Jealousy
ORANGE: Deaf & Dumb
BROWN: Spirit of Bondage
BLACK: Spirit of anti-Christ

NUMBER 8

Pray over all manifestations and command everything to leave. Invite the Holy Spirit to come in and occupy.

THE SPIRITS THAT COMBINE TOGETHER
TO CAUSE APOSTASY

This group is a combination of the spirits involved in Jealousy, the spirits involved in the Deaf and Dumb and then the spirits involved in Apostasy. It is anarchy.

For this combination the pattern repeats. All primaries are included, all secondarys and brown - Bondage. Follow the order on the mix shown on Jealousy and then pray for the Deaf and Dumb to leave. Then pray over the Spirit of Whoredom.

Finally, command that unclean Bondage to leave. At work are the groups that causes divorce, the group that causes suicide, unteachable spirit, severe depression and mental illness, and the group that causes apathy and severe poverty.

Children are especially victimized - rebellion, divorce, suicide, backwards thinking, and a seeking after the world becomes their inheritance. This spirit is a devouring lion that robs, steals and destroys.

Of special interest in this area is the controlling and manipulation - lots of game playing and power plays.

Purple is a family relationship color. Check for bitter roots. Also pay particular attention to the family skeletons or "Family Familiars". Make a list of your own family sin that repeats from generation to generation (witchcraft, incest, alcoholism, etc.).

Pray and place the Cross between your family and your mother and father and between your family and your husband's mother and father for the last four generations and command that sin to come to the Cross and stop!

Another area to check is the breach, which is the unnecessary breaking of friendships. Also include love of the world and love of social position.

Pray against the holds of Bondage, stomp around and do warfare until those snakes leave.

Under Whoredom, evil poses as good, with excessive love of the world, or of self. New Ageism and Humanism could be categorized as being directed by the Spirit of Whoredom as could excessive self-hate. Whoredom is self or worldly worship.

<u>Jesus</u> The King of Kings

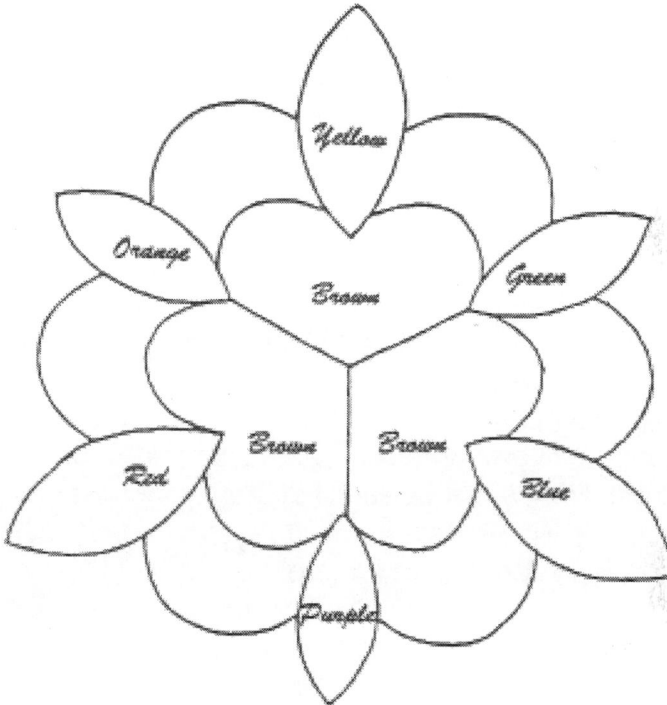

STRONGMEN 9   APOSTASY / WHOREDOM

WHITE:	Lying Spirit
YELLOW:	Proud and Haughty / Spirit of Infirmity
RED:	Spirit of Perversion and Divination
BLUE:	Spirit of Fear and Heaviness
GREEN:	Spirit of Jealousy
ORANGE:	Deaf & Dumb
PURPLE:	Spirit of Whoredom
BROWN:	Spirit of Bondage
BLACK:	Spirit of anti-Christ

NUMBER 9

Pray over all manifestations and command everything leave.

THE HEART OF THE CHART

The heart of the chart is an area you will want to pray for after you have prayed over each combination or group. When you pray for each area of bondage to leave you are actually breaking a dirty, unclean spirit. When this spirit leaves you literally take the land.

Each section of the heart has to be taken individually. The first piece of land you win, number one, is the *Homeland* and it is the combination of the spirit that comes to cause divorce and division. The leader is Jealousy.

Number two, the second heart you can take is the Deaf and Dumb. The Deaf and Dumb steals your hopes and dreams. When you break this part of bondage you restore *The Land of your Hopes and Dreams.*

The third heart is the area that causes Whoredom. The leader is the Spirit of Whoredom: the Proud and Haughty and the Spirit of Infirmity. These spirits destroy your finances and your relationship with God the Father and your health. They keep you living by worldly standards where true prosperity can never really happen. When you destroy this power you release yourself to financial and physical blessing into the land of God's provision - the land of purple - *The Promise Land.*

In the Bible God foreshadows our move from the wilderness into the promise land. The Jews first stepped into this promise land when they came out of their forty year journey in the wilderness. They entered the land of Canaan (Joshua 1). Even today the land of Canaan is called the land of purple. It was where all the purple dyes were produced.

So when we break this spirit we, too, can enter into the land of Canaan, our land of purple, our *Promise Land.*

Know when you finish praying spiritual warfare you do not become perfect, but it allows you to be a cleaner vessel for the perfect which is Jesus. It allows you to enter into the real battle - the battle for the Kingdom to come in the lives of others and here on earth. It builds a base of spiritual discernment from which to see and hear the battle more clearly.

Promise Land

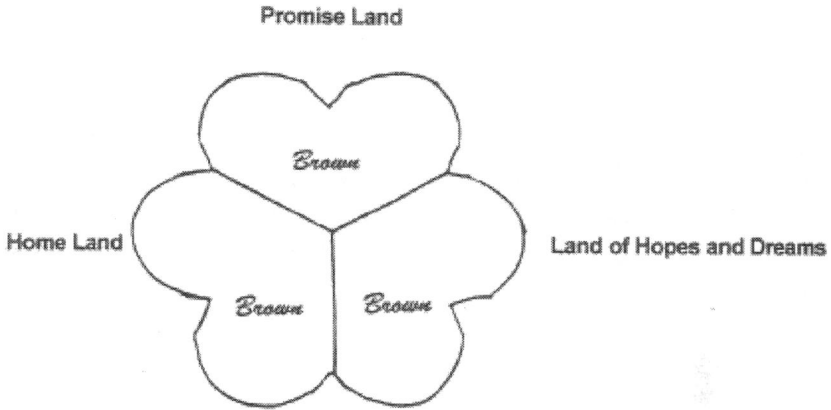

Home Land

Land of Hopes and Dreams

The heart of the chart is simply the middle of the colorwheel. Brown represents the lands that we take as we overcome in each area. These lands are spiritual lands. Ownership of our own land determines the authroity we have to take land for others.

Training Manual for Land Ownership

Review ~ The Color of the Lie
Revelation 9:17

Spirits can work singly or in groups. When they work in groups you must deal with all the spirits one-by-one included in that group.

0-9   LYING SPIRIT - The little white lie
        Strong delusions,
        White contains all colors

1   HAUGHTY SPIRIT - Yellow
        INFIRMITY - Yellow
        Proud, bragging, egotistical,
        bitterness, arthritis, disease
        dictatorial, controlling

2   PERVERSION - Red
        SPIRIT OF DIVINATION Red
        Lust, sexual perversion,
        rebellion, witchcraft,
        to pervert the Gospel,
        familiar spirits

3   FEAR - Blue
        HEAVINESS - Blue
        Fright, dead, torment,
        mourning, despair,
        inferiority, depression

3   DEAF AND DUMB - Orange
        Insanity, Suicide and an
        unteachable spirit

4   JEALOUSY - Green
     Division, murder,
     coveting, suspicion

5   WHOREDOM - Purple
     Love of self, love of the world,
     love of social position, love of
     power

6   BONDAGE - Brown
     Satanic Captivity

0-9 THE SPIRIT OF ANTI-CHRIST
     Black is a combination of everything.

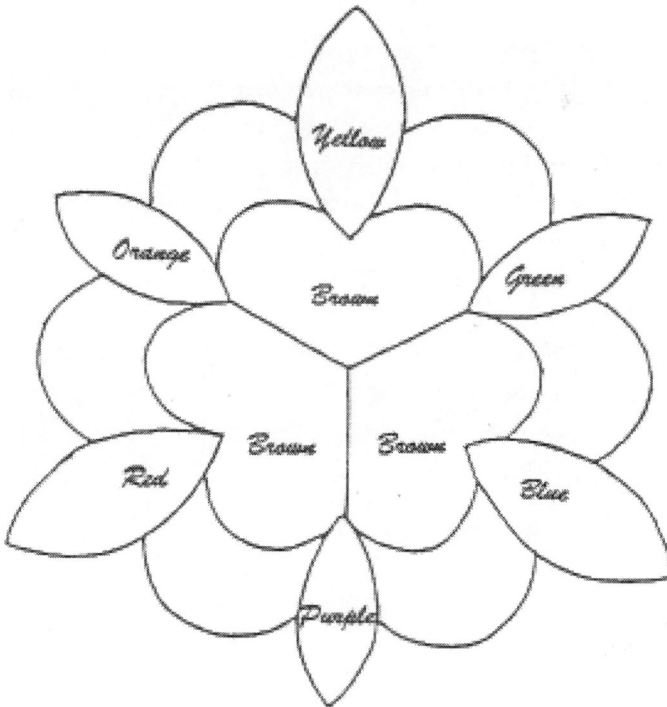

When Spirits Combine to Form Groups

DIVORCE - lack of harmony
KEY - I will not!
Combination of all primaries
and the secondary jealousy,
then pray over Bondage.

DEAF AND DUMB - The lack of sanity
KEY - I am nothing!
Combination of all
primaries and the two
secondarys. The Deaf and
Dumb is the leader.
Now pray over Bondage.

WHOREDOM - Total debauchery, worldliness:
Key - I am the center of everything!
God is nothing!
Combination of all primaries
and all secondarys with Whoredom
as the leader.
Finally, pray over Bondage.

The following pages are called the Exodus Journal and are a prayer journal for you to track your deliverance journey. At the end of the Exodus Journal you will find a personal word from Pastor MaryJo Lovelady.

Training Manual for Land Ownership

6
The Exodus Journal

The Exodus Journal

The Exodus Journal

The Exodus Journal

The Exodus Journal

The Exodus Journal

The Exodus Journal

The Exodus Journal

The Exodus Journal

The Exodus Journal

The Exodus Journal

The Exodus Journal

The Exodus Journal

The Exodus Journal

The Exodus Journal

The Exodus Journal

THE LAST WORD

Deliverance is not the end of God's process. You must maintain your deliverance.

When an unclean spirit goes out of a man, he goes through dry places seeking rest and finds none. Then he says " I will return to my house from which I came", and when he comes he finds it empty, swept and put into order. Then he goes and takes with him seven other spirits more wicked than himself and they enter and dwell there; and the last state of the man is worse than the first. So shall it be with this wicked generation (Matthew 12:43-45).

Jesus sums it up by saying, *See you have been made well. Sin no more lest a worse thing come upon you (John 5:14).*

Then how do we maintain our deliverance? First of all we must make Jesus the Lord of our life. Lord means supreme authority. When Jesus is Lord of our life that means He rules and reigns. There is no room for another king! First and foremost in your life must be the Lordship of Jesus. *Confess with your mouth the Lord Jesus (Romans 10:9).*

Secondly, you must be quick to confess sin. In I John 1:9 we find that if we confess our sins, He is faithful and just to forgive our sin and to cleanse us from all unrighteousness.

What is unrighteousness? The definition of unrighteousness is misdeeds, injustice, moral wrong doing, unjust actions. It is the opposite of truthfulness, faithfulness and righteousness. Be quick to admit and confess your sin.

This brings us to the next step in maintaining deliverance. We must be forgiving and be forgiven. That is just what Jesus said in the Lord's Prayer in Matthew 6: 9-15 when He was teaching His disciples how to pray. In verse 12 He defines how we obtain forgiveness, *"forgive us our debts as we forgive our debtors."*

It was so important that two verses later Jesus repeats the lesson.

For if you forgive men their trespasses, your heavenly Father will also forgive you. But if you do not forgive men their trespasses, neither will your Father forgive your trespasses Matthew 6:9-15).

You may not feel like forgiving but it is an action of your will, a decision you make, a choice not dependant upon your emotions or how you feel.

And of course, the most important step you can ever take is knowing the Lord Jesus personally. How do we know Him? We know Him through His Word. In Matthew 4:1-10 Jesus Himself defeats the devil through quoting Scripture. Take the example Jesus has set for keeping the devil away. Know the Word of God and use it! Notice how Jesus used Scripture as He spoke to the devil, *"Away with you, Satan! For it is written..."* Then Jesus quoted a Scripture pertaining to the temptation.

The evil one was trying to get Jesus to worship him. The Scripture Jesus quoted against the enemy with success was, *"You shall worship the Lord your God and Him only shall you serve!"* The very next verse states, *"Then the devil left Him!"*

In Ephesians we find a final step to keeping deliverance.

Be filled with the Spirit, speaking to one another in psalms and hymns and spiritual songs, singing and making melody in your heart to the Lord (Ephesians 5:18).

Follow these steps to be a happy and free Christian!
Pastor Maryjo Lovelady

Spiritual Strength Training Series
THE KINGDOM - CHRISTIAN PRIMARY I $13.00

This book offers a comprehensive overview of God's Kingdom and Kingdom prayers. It includes basic Kingdom structure, practical applications of love, faith and hope, healing and inner healing. 9x6 ISBN 0-9718325-0-1

The Kingdom Teacher's Manual $31.00

Developed by a veteran teacher, this easy to use teacher's guide for *The Kingdom* offers chapter study guides, 20 pages of hands-on activities, a treasure map and art front plates from the four Gospels. 8 1/2x11 ISBN 0-9718325-3-6

The Revolution Begins - THE KINGDOM JOURNAL $13.00

The Kingdom Journal is a Student Handbook/Workbook for participants in their study of *The Kingdom*. It is the companion text to *The Kingdom Teacher's Manual* containing Journal sheets for dreams, visions and words from God and all the necessary handout materials from *The Kingdom Teacher's Manual*. 8 1/2x11 ISBN 0-9718325-9-5

Wonderland -THE KINGDOM Music CD $10.00

THE GLORY - CHRISTIAN PRIMARY II $13.00

Jesus is the Glory and the light of the world. Man was created to walk in the light of the Glory of God. *The Glory* explore colors, numbers and the anointing of King, Priest and Prophet using color as a visual aid. 9x6 ISBN 0-9718325-1-X

The Glory Color Book COLORING BOOK $10.00

Imaginative color book to reinforce *The Glory* 8 1/2x11 ISBN 0-9718325-4-4

The Year of the Lyger -POWERPOINT CD $13.00

Must have companion material for *The Glory*. The Lion and the Tiger release prophetic art for the King, priest and prophet. 8 1/2x11 Lyger prints $30.00 each

THE POWER - CHRISTIAN PRIMARY III $13.00

The Power offers a practical guide to knowing the Holy Spirit and practicing deliverance. It teaches on deliverance and how to recognize enemy spirits through the language they speak. 9x6 ISBN 0-9718325-2-8

The Sound of Deliverance-POWERPOINT CD $13.00

Powerpoint presentation of all prayers from *The Kingdom, The Glory and The Power*. Plus more!!!

Rumors of Nard: The Book of 7,8, and 9 $13.00

Compelling allegory of Deliverance. 9x6 ISBN 0-9718325-7-9

Order your Spiritual Strength Training Series Today!

1 (503) 791-1922

·

7243637R0

Made in the USA
Charleston, SC
08 February 2011